For my beautiful daughter Meádhbh &

My Angel son John Raymond.

About The Author:

Seán Ó Sirideán was born in Newry and reared in the south Armagh border village of Bessbrook in county Armagh.

He has been writing songs and poetry since he was a young boy, writing about the beautiful landscape that he grew up around and about the people and local characters that he met along the way.

After working for the BBC for seven years he is now working on a new stage play about the Magdalene Laundries set in 1960's Newry.

For all enquires visit www.seanosiridean.com

Forward By Tom Flannery:

I'm an American. From Scranton, PA to be precise. Plenty of good Irish-catholic folk around these parts. We dream in the colours of the Irish tricolour, drain $5 Guinness pints by the gallon, sing along to the Clancy Brothers, and have our own St. Patrick's Day parade, the excuse we definitely do not need to wear green and get drunk. We curse those Brits, own a copy of "The Quiet Man" on DVD, and grow misty-eyed over the plight of Bobby Sands. We can trace our families back to the old country, many of them chased here by the hunger of the 1840s. My family came from Sligo and Mayo, respectively. They made their way here with little more than the clothes on their back, and assimilated through the sheer force of their Gaelic personality. Just thinking about all of this makes me want to put on a Chieftains record and start quoting James Joyce. It's very romantic and all that, you see.

It's also a fraud, of course. I'm about as Irish as John Wayne, who was born in Iowa. But that doesn't stop me from gazing across the sea with longing, burning with fever from the words I've read and the stills I've seen and those Jim Sheridan films I've pirated for constant re-viewing. For that's what Ireland does. It makes you feel its terrible beauty even when you have as much chance of living there as on Sesame Street.

Seán Ó Sirideán is my mate. Lives in Belfast. A lovely writer. Wonderful singer. A man with a twinkle in his heart. A man who can feel the lash when it's applied to others. A man with the soul of a lion. When I read this collection, I hear music between these words. Because Sean writes both for the eye and the ear, a delicate balance that he pulls off wonderfully here. Sean is a complex, driven bloke who communicates with a disarming simplicity. And if you think that's easy, ask yourself why so few others can do the same.

He has taught me more about Ireland, in this slender volume, than the whole of Joyce's Ulysses. If this sounds crazy, may I remind you that Sean is very good and that the only Americans who claim to understand what Joyce is rambling on about are liars.

I delight in Sean's recollections of childhood, the mad mates and memories of days we lose only when we die. I delight in his ramblings around Bessbrook, a place where ghosts can outnumber the living. I can feel the flame that still emanates from his Republican comrades. And when I got to the part where his neighbour Micky Mallon threatens to x-ray him "to see if there's any work in you", I spit out what constitutes tea in America in a howl of laughter.

I'm reminded all over again why I love Ireland. And why I don't mind being fraudulent, because I've got a direct link back there. Friendship does that for you.

-- Tom Flannery

January 2017
Scranton PA

Lonely Streets Of Ghosts

(For The Green Road Residents Past & Present)

I'll tell a little story, about a simple road.
A street just outside Bessbrook,
Where the craic it once did flow.

This place it is called Green Road, a warm, loving place at most.
But now to me it has become
A lonely street of ghosts.

I smell Annie's toffee apples,
As I say hello to Mr Quinn.
A little wave to Minnie,
As she tends her garden till.

Miriah and John Doherty,
Fine people I can say.
And lovely Mrs Mooney,
At the window, night and day.

I never did meet Harry,
But I'm told he was a gent.
And with his Stewartstown sweetheart
To the Green Road there they went.

I'll never forget sweet Mrs Carroll
And the bold oul 'Skipper' true.
The gentle Bernadette, Phil and Seamus too.

Young Richard he did leave us,
And it was all too soon.
He looks upon number 78

From the stars and from the moon.

JB, Una, Rory- that amazing boy to all.
His smile it was infectious
And he loved to play football.

Packy, Eamon, Mrs Hughes,
Jim Bra sadly gone away. And dear old Margaret McLaughlin
Who always had the time of day.

Now sadly I must recollect the ones that I come from.
James Niall, Nanny, Mary- she was the special one.

The lady of the Green Road was a girl named Gloria Anne,
Her husband's name was Seán,
A loving family man.

So, as I look upon it, Green Road, to you I toast.
But sadly all you are to me
Is a lonely street of ghosts.

Cavehill

Cavehill looks over north Belfast

Like the keeper of the gate.

With Napoleon's nose so vibrant

It has damn near sealed my fate.

If atop that massive rock front

All of Belfast looks so small.

I can see the yellow cranes in east

And all the writing on the wall.

Over west I see Black Mountain,

Poleglass, Lenadoon, Andytown.

And scanning over eastward –

There's the star, the county Down.

I can see Ballymacarrett,

The staunch and free Short Strand.

From atop this Cavehill Mountain

I can see most of this land.

Rebel Heads & Big Cow Sheds

I'm from south Armagh

Where the hills are fresh and green.

Where the air is blue with splendour

With a beauty not much seen.

It's where Rebel heads meet big cow sheds

On any country road.

And giants thread on ancient soil

Crying out their warrior code.

Gaelic culture thrives here,

In sport and in song.

And the blackbird chirps her ditty

To carry her listeners along.

To be here is to love here

And sometimes, love is hard to bare.

But as you gaze upon Sliabh gCuircín

You cannot help but care.

As the autumnal sunlight sparkles

Upon Bessbrook's lonely pond

It's then I know I'm home now

As it holds me with its bond.

Yeah, it's where Rebel heads meet big cow sheds

On any country road.

Farewell to Derry

For Martin McGuinness

It's been a few hours since I learned that Martin died.

We mourn his death sorely all over Ireland wide.

A man who fought for Ireland and n'er a knee did bend

As he led his country onward and a message he did send.

The Bogside was his hometown, a town he loved so well.

From the lowlands of the Creggan to his beloved Brandywell.

Born into political hatred, a gerrymandered state.

He struck a blow for Ireland and sealed our country's fate.

As a soldier of dear Ireland, he led with head on high.

If you chanced upon the Creggan you'd hear his battle cry.

May the Inishowen Peninsula An Grianan hold his soul

As the Northern winds blow softly crying Ireland's freedom goal.

Fairy Tree

The Fairy Tree in Bessbrook,

Is a place where fairies play.

They do twinkle in the sunlight,

And glint upon the moon.

As they flutter to and forth,

As they sing and as they croon.

Oh that little Fairy Tree,

As it looks upon the pond.

And where fairies take their shelter

While they hold a loving bond.

There's a flock of fairies floating

To the Crow's Walk they do fly.

As a low fog captures Bessbrook yet they glint upon the sky.

So you little fairy people,

Who do look upon us all.

And you scatter for your branches

When you hear the Banshee call.

As your Fairy Tree sways gently

Let it always be at ease.

As it shudders on the pond path

In a fresh south Armagh breeze.

Shaun's Dilemma

(For Gary Anderson, Sean & Michael Keenan)

The fawn bitch of 'The Brook' she was an enigma.

Lightning fast greyhound the bold Shaun's Dilemma.

Trained and reared in a modest Armagh garden,

She breezed past all others with not but a pardon.

For as day turns to night the hound chases Hare,

Be in dark Monaghan hedgerows or Ennis in Clare.

Shaun's Dilemma ears pinned back and on like a flash,

As the crowds look in wonder at her frightening fast dash.

Rarely did she visit the ancient Clonmel.

Without cup and glory that suited her well.

As she earned admiration she was never mistook

As she strolled home from victory to her homeland Bessbrook.

Childhood Superstitions

I had a funny feeling,

That went straight through my head.

About how years ago,

When I was young –

Dandelions were 'Piss the beds.'

Or how little yellow buttercups,

Could surely start a flutter.

As you held them underneath your chin –

To tell if you liked butter.

When every time we did all play,

And we might just hear a cry.

We were convinced it was the old Banshee.

Announcing you're to die.

Now Roy he was a neighbour,

And he owned a Billy Goat.

And if he were to catch you –

He'd wear you as a coat.

These childhood superstitions,

Still fondly I can tell.

Folklore and old traditions –

Stood generations very well.

Duncairn Dander

The unmistakable smell of freshly cut grass,

Hits me like a bolt of lightening

As I meander through Duncairn on a dawn morning.

The dew still dancing as the sun catches it

Unaware of its splendour.

Having no destination, only a will to walk for

The fear of sleep and the demons therein

Make rest and slumber a proposition inconsiderable.

I hear swans and ducks craw and make their morning noise

As if to yawn aloud and welcome the new day

As I sit and watch on Belfast's Waterworks under the watchful

Gaze of Napoleon and his nose upon historic Cavehill.

A fine and misty rain comes in from due east and dampens

The new morning though not my moment as I take deep breath again,

Smell the morning drizzle and feel the love of nature engulf me.

An ode to Bessbrook

The green low fields of Bessbrook, I often long to see.

The ancient standing stones, which are always home to me.

Sweet winding Green Road beauty, where legends grew to be,

Just off the Camlough main road, where I often dream to be.

Higher up above, great High Street, looking down on us below,
As the sun shines down McGinn's field, as the cattle eat and grow.

Down the Boiler Hill, around Crow's Walk, through the pond, into the 'Brook',
as I stood in that model village, the breath of me it took.

Now I live far away in the city lights, the sun, I never see it set,
But the sun it shines bright over Bessbrook, that small village, I'll never forget.

Love They Cannot Kill

For Éamonn Ceannt

I dreamt I heard your voice last night.

You wrapped your arms around me and embraced me oh so tight.

We kissed and embraced like many times before.

Its then I was awoken by the sound of my prison door.

For that one moment love, we were together still.

And as I walk to death this morn, that memory they cannot kill.

For our love knows no prison, it knows no walls of hate.

It only knows my love for you, and for Ireland now my fate.

Connecticut To Here
For Neva

Sitting in the cool, crisp gardens of Belfast's Botanic.
Watching as songbirds play me one more tune before
I pick the sweetest rose.

Only a shadow for comfort or touch
And then heartache does appear.
But that's the love I held one time –
It's in Connecticut to here.

The blonde hair like curtains,
Letting me peer at her natural beauty.
Eyes so kind and gentle that even the
Toughest heart would surely relent.

As I sit alone in Belfast, looking at her photos dear
And suddenly I remember that love –
It's in Connecticut to here.

My memory deceives me still –
As during daily mundanity she flashes through my mind.
Maybe only a single word, a laugh.
Any small refrain reminds me of her.

Often when the wind blows hard
And the trees howl sad with fear.
It's then I'll think about that one sweet love –
It's in Connecticut to here.

My eyes filled with tears today,
When Finbar sang the lines –
"One aimless walk & My Belfast love"
As all I could think about was her.

Damn this ocean so wide and so blue,

For it cuts me from her fair heart.
But my heart's like an island –
Strong and sincere.
Oh I never will forget that love.
It came from Connecticut to here.

Remembrance of Chimney Smoke

I get terrible pangs of reminiscence

When I smell chimney smoke.

Do you remember coal, doubles, peat,

And white paraffin fire lighters?

I remember every morning, hearing my Granny

Clean out the fire grate;

The noise shook the floor boards.

And getting bags of sticks to help light

The damp coal from the back shed.

Toasting bread over a hot open fire

Was a favourite Sunday pastime as a boy.

Crack! The dry wood would awaken

And panic would ensue to get the fire guard in place.

Old newspapers crunched up

To serve as make do tinder

Today I walked past a house with

Bellows of grey smoke oozing from the chimney.

The smell brought me back to easier, simpler days,

When life was easy and free.

Some Old Man in Some Old Pub

I often see him sitting on the same chair,

In the same public house,

With the same glass of stout and Power's malt

With tumbler of tap water to make the sting

Of the whisky a little more pleasing

Even for his well versed pallet.

Cloth cap and Player's cigarettes unfiltered

Strong enough to rattle the sturdiest of lungs.

He read's his Irish News in between sips.

He lifts his head to look at the horse racing results

On which he inevitably lost his Each Way bet,

Sighs, and goes again.

I can't help but notice his startling green eyes

That has no doubt saw things that my young soul

Could only ever dare to even dream of.

Olé Olé Summer 1990

Often times I recall summer 1990.

As a 10 year old boy singing Olé Olé Olé.

I was certain we would win the World Cup

As Big Jack would lead the way.

Myself and neighbour Philip

Painting faces green, white and gold.

When we drew with them ones, England

We knew Ireland ner would fold.

Beating Romania in the shoot out

Packie Bonar Saved the day

And we cheered and cried for Ireland

As our boys they trailed the way.

The Italians and Schillaci

Just too good that day we met.

But that summer 1990

A summer Ireland won't forget.

The Man Inside The Paining

The man inside the painting

He is standing to the fore.

And flanked by other soldiers

For Ireland evermore.

The scene is in the Square,

South Armagh's chosen men.

Led by McNamee

From the fighting Crossmaglen.

He faced Britain bravely,

And never knee did bend.

As he roamed the ancient trenches

For his homeland to defend.

A man so unassuming,

But his flame of freedom ran.

When he told me of McAllister's

Daffodil man from Kiltybane.

The man inside the painting,

He is a friend you see.

The man inside the painting

My friend Pat McNamee.

Session in the Railway

Every Thursday there's a session
In Newry's Railway Bar.
Where fine tunes are played
From within near and far.

Terry Conlon on accordion
He'd bellow out a tune.
While we listened quite intently
There is silence in the room.

Robbie Doolin on Bouzouki sings
'My Little Dublin Girl'
And I close my eyes and see her
Dublin beauty there unfurled.

Ruairí then brings out the guitar
And he tells about 'Beeswing'
How she sat White Horse in pocket
That Meigh man can surely sing.

As the mighty tunes go faster

And our hearts begin to swell.

We think of Mickey Cunnane boys,

And the craic to us he'd tell.

That's a session in the Railway

Flutes and fiddles, stories told.

And the craic it sure is 90

On the low lying Camlough road.

The Greedy Keeper Of The Jewel

Watch her greedily guard our jewel.

Self-absorbed, attention hungry.

Keeper of the stone.

Only she can have control over the diamond –

For she has stolen the precious gem

With the benevolence that becomes her.

Power of ownership goes to her head.

Making her drunk with control as she

Sweeps away any suggestions that may weaken

Her position of importance.

Civility is a luxury she seems to neglect

As she holds the gemstone in front of you,

Only for a slight moment while running off

With her devilish grin.

But, time waits for no man or woman.

The diamond she holds will too mature with time.

And, like all precious stones will make her own journey

Back to the Promised Land of síocháin.

Toffee Apples Annie

Like Bees around sweet nectar

We all gathered around Annie and Homer's House.

Her famous toffee apples where the highlight of all our ghostly hallows

On Bessbrook's Green Road.

An Army of children were sent to pick up any discarded ice-lolly sticks

So as Annie would never run out of handles for her sweetest of treats.

They sold for 50p, but she gave them all away,

To any child that came calling for Annie's toffee apples.

Eileen

(Ode to first love)

One never forgets ones first true love

Mine was a girl called Eileen.

If truth be told, I never loved another

Quite since then and probably never will.

From 'courtin' around the Pond Field

And holding hands on walks to nowhere

Only where our feet desired to go.

Talking of life's dreams, future hopes

And endless nights of holding hands

And sweet refrains.

She possessed the bluest eyes which held

Small white stars carved carefully in each pupil

They still send shivers down my back.

Her soul was gentle with an almost innocence-

From within exploding outward

Through those expressive, star filled eyes.

When she held my hand, I knew then

Nothing else mattered at that moment.

Everything was good with the world.

A childhood sweetheart, my only true love,

Slipped through my childish fingers

On a day I'd rather forget.

Tricky Micky Mallon

I had a neighbour, Micky Mallon

A sort of a Del Boy if you will.

He would buy you once and sell you twice

If you ever stood so still.

I remember Micky was a hardworking man,

Always looking for the next pound.

If it wasn't in the chip van

Then you'd hear the ice-cream van sound.

He had freezers from Jamaica,

Cookers from Brazil,

He'd sell ice-cream to the Eskimos

If they'd open up their till.

I was never one for working,

I'd rather sit and drink cups of tay.

It was then one day Micky told me

I'm taking you for an X-Ray.

When I asked what for? He told me;

"To see if there's any work in you"

That's how I remember Micky Mallon

And I smile each time I do.

Rubicon

Oh to cross the Rubicon

That famous water stretch by Rome.

For to reach ones last endeavour

To hopefully find ones way back home.

For to fight a way through Rubicon,

Water shallow in my heart.

To see your sallow pale face,

Hold you; never be apart.

Maybe fly over the Rubicon,

To look down from on the stars.

Your long, blonde hair reflecting

To be seen from here to Mars.

Now let's close this long Rubicon.

Hold my hand over the Strand.

We can lay and sleep together

As we seep into the land.

Camlough Mountain

As you dander hence from Newry

Many miles for it to see.

The sweeping Camlough Mountain

Cast a shadow over thee.

Many years she was a prisoner

Of a foreign cruel woe.

But now that they have left her

The people own her so.

She has looked upon the village

And inspired folk to dream.

She has cloaked herself in low cloud

While she blazed in sun soaked beam.

It's a mountain cast in beauty

That only God could make.

And there to quench her deep thirst

Is the spellbound Camlough Lake.

So Sliabh gCuircín as you're standing

Brave and bold for evermore.

As you offer us your shelter

You are etched upon the core.

Rainy Night In Belfast

It's a rainy night in Belfast,

The clouds come tumbling in.

As all around the New Lodge –

No noise, no sound, no din.

The cold rain batters my face

As I look up to the sky.

And then I think of Bessbrook

My God, I want to cry.

The coldness of this city

It eats away my soul.

If it wasn't for my shadow

I'd forever be alone.

It's a rainy night in Belfast,

And the chill my bones it shook.

And I sit alone in New Lodge,

Thinking of you, sweet Bessbrook.

Ballykeel Dolmen

As a cool damp south Armagh mist

Dissented upon the Ballykeel Dolmen.

I stood in footsteps of my Stone Age ancestors

And quietly drank in the beauty.

The magnificent statue like burial ground

Of ancient people brings one to ponder.

How did such primitive people most massive granite?

Why? Where from? But more importantly who?

We see those Stone Age folk

Every time we look into a mirror.

They were here long before and

Will be here long after we've gone.

Just like at Kilnasagart and Drumsill

Reminders of our history and our people

Carved in ancient stone.

Drunken Morning Woods Walk

Took an early morning half-drunk stroll

Through the Bessbrook woods.

A place I hadn't been since childhood.

Walks and courting expeditions.

As I felt the autumnal leaves crunch

Underneath my feet,

Mother Nature whispered to me 'Let it go.'

Let these broken leaves be your broken soul.

As if by the hand of a higher power

Wind swept around me, lifting golden fresh leaves

Telling me somehow to keep walking, to discover more.

Majestic feelings of earthly homebound

Soothing voices echoed around that sparse wood.

There, I left some of my pain and walked free.

Lament to Seán Doran

Under Shadows of Sliabh gCuircín

Camlough village sits at ease.

As Seán Doran walks Louth wards,

Cutting through the Armagh breeze.

As he served his country bravely

And stood fast by Aiken's side

He trailed from Cross to Forkhill

Fighting Britain's mighty tide.

He was struck down by a coward

In the back by British lead

But they never can besmirch you

Rest in peace in your soldier's bed.

A gentle soul who love his homeland

And who struck for freedoms might

Seán Doran we remember you

In the cold, dark Camlough night.

Still The Cold Night

Still the cold air that settles here tonight.

With low mist fleeting forth

Shows an eerie Irish sight.

To the long stretch of green grass

That suckles fresh sweet dew.

By abandoned lovers walk ways

That where thread upon by few.

Ripples of echoes past now stretch

From here to there.

As the blackbird sings his heartache

All along this empty Irish air.

Brown leaves fall upon the footpath

As the bitter winds do chill.

And that echo from my loud cry

Can be heard on Convent Hill.

To then look around the sparseness

Is a broken sight to see.

For this is what I am now –

No room to run or flee.

Wimbledon on Green Road

Wimbledon started and overnight
We all became tennis fans.

Days spent playing tennis over our front gate
Andre Agassi was on Green Road daily.

There was me, Frank, Bra, Anthony, Raymie,
Philip and Paddy.
Sports stars of yesterday, but I was the best,
Obviously.

Arguments over what balls were
In and what balls were out.
As the chalked lines seemed to move
And sway to suit the bigger lad.

Simpler days, when Wimbledon was on Green Road.

The Forgotten Fallen Women Of Newry

In a convent outside Newry

'Fallen women' are to go.

Their souls they are not pure enough

And for why they do not know.

These Nuns they call it charity

These poor women are at loss.

As they use their whips for punishment

Jesus weeps upon his cross.

'Oh Sister please don't hurt me

I am barley even ten.'

But the Bride of Christ looks through her

And the belt comes out again.

Nora Ann is sent to the laundry

At 14 years what was her crime?

She was raped and then fell pregnant

So to them she was but slime.

As she sorely suffered labour

Her baby girl wrapped in a coat

She never got to hold her

As they put her on a boat.

For a new born is worth money

To rich Americans abroad.

These nuns dare call it charity

Christ its nothing but a fraud.

An Evening Walk With Patsy

An evening walk with Patsy,

Around Divernagh we would stray.

And talk about the country,

And the state it's in today.

As we reached the Ballynabee

And the convent down below.

We would talk about Our Lady

How the grace that she would show.

As we passed through Cambrook Park

For Camlough we did make.

We spoke about old Ireland

And how she's ours to take.

When we reached St. Malachy's Park

Mrs McCreesh had kettle boiled.

And she'd tell me about Dorsey

Of how they farmed and worked and toiled.

I can still hear Jimmy's laugh,

As we sat around the fire.

And the love he had for Susan

It was something to admire.

Sadly now these days are over,

But my heart may never fret.

For an evening walk with Patsy,

Memories never to forget.

Love Letter To A Daughter

(For Meádhbh)

Dear daughter, just a few lines

To say I love you so.

Don't ever be afraid

Daddy's always where you go.

Dear daughter, just a few lines

You make me proud each day.

No matter what life gives you

Keep on going your own way.

Dear daughter, just a few lines

Your face so fresh and kind.

Your eyes they stare straight through me

They are burned deep in my mind.

Dear daughter, just a few lines

To remind you Daddy's here.

And he'll always be here waiting

To hold you close so dear.

Seán Ó Sirideán's long anticipated debut
collection of poems

THE RAMBLINGS OF A BESSBROOK BOY

Seán Ó Sirideán

www.ingramcontent.com/pod-product-compliance
Ingram Content Group UK Ltd.
Pitfield, Milton Keynes, MK11 3LW, UK
UKHW022201110125
453409UK00011B/356